Bedtime Bible

Bedtime Bible

Stephanie Jeffs

Illustrated by Graham Round

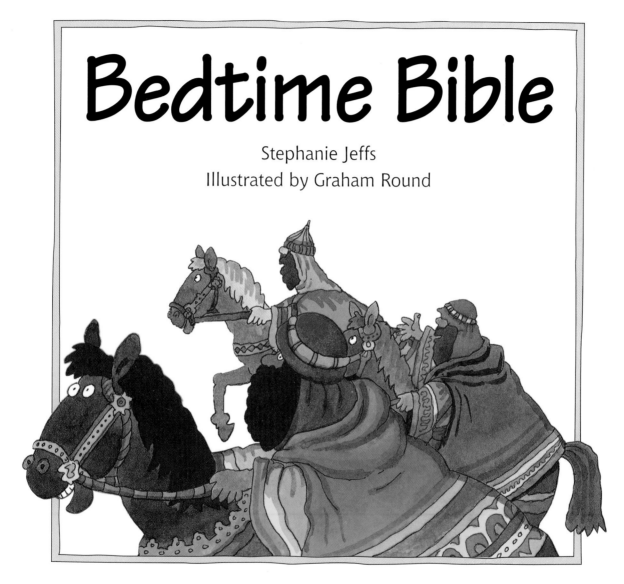

Marshall Pickering

An Imprint of HarperCollins*Publishers*

Marshall Pickering is an imprint of
HarperCollins*Religious*
Part of HarperCollins*Publishers*
77-85 Fulham Palace Road, London W6 8JB

First published in Great Britain in 1999 by Marshall Pickering

1 3 5 7 9 10 8 6 4 2

Copyright © 1999 AD Publishing Services Ltd
1 Churchgates, The Wilderness, Berkhamsted, Herts HP4 2UB
Illustrations © 1999 Graham Round

Stephanie Jeffs asserts the moral right to be identified as the author of this work.
A catalogue record for this book is available from the British Library.

ISBN 0 551 03218 9

Printed and bound in Singapore

Introduction

For generations, parents and grandparents have told and read the stories of the Bible to their children. This collection of Bible stories has been especially written to introduce young children to the Bible, its people and its message.

The forty-two illustrated stories have been selected to take the child through the 'one story' of the Bible, from the creation, through Noah, Abraham, Moses and David to the life of Jesus and the beginnings of the Christian church.

Each story is complete in itself and is accompanied by a simple prayer, offering a perfect way to end the day.

Contents

God makes the world

In the beginning there was nothing at all.
Only God was there.

God made everything we see around us.
God made the light and the darkness.
He made big, tall mountains, and deep blue seas.
God made plants and flowers and trees. He filled the
land with them.

God made the round, spinning earth, the red hot sun

and the silvery moon. He made the twinkling stars and planets.

Then God filled the sea with slippery, shiny fish and the air with birds that chatter and sing. God made animals that leap and clamber and crawl on the land.

God was pleased with everything he had made. It was very good.

'Now I will make some people,' said God. So he made the first man and woman. They were called Adam and Eve.

God wanted them to enjoy his world. He wanted them to be happy. God loved them very much. He made a beautiful garden for them to live in. It was called the garden of Eden.

"Thank you, God, for the beautiful world you have given us!"

The enemy in the garden

Adam and Eve were very happy living in the beautiful garden.

God asked them to choose names for the animals and to take care of them. The garden was full of delicious fruits and vegetables, and they could eat anything they wanted, except from one tree.

There was a big tree in the middle of the garden. 'It is called the tree of knowing good and bad,' said God. 'You mustn't eat any of its fruit. If you do, everything will be spoiled.'

One day God's enemy came into the garden. He didn't like the beautiful garden and he wanted to spoil all the things God had made and planned.

He crept up to Eve and hissed in her ear. 'God was lying when he told you about that tree. You won't die if you eat its fruit. You will be great, just like God!'

Eve looked at the tree.
The fruit looked so delicious.
She took a big, deep bite. Then she
gave some to Adam.

Suddenly they knew what they had done. The garden
didn't look the same any more. They didn't feel the same
any more. Everything was spoiled. They had disobeyed
God.

God was very sad. 'Because you did not do what I
said,' he told them, 'you will have to leave.'

And so they left the beautiful garden.

"Dear God, I'm sorry
that sometimes I
do things that are
wrong. I am
sorry that it makes
you sad."

Noah builds a boat

The world had become a very unhappy place. People were fighting and arguing all the time. They had all forgotten about God.

When God saw how bad everyone was, it made him very, very sad. He began to wish that he had never made the world.

But there was one man who still loved God. His name was Noah. Noah tried to do what God wanted; and God was very pleased with him.

One day, God spoke to Noah. 'I wish I had never made the world,' he said. 'I am going to start again. I am going to flood the earth with water, and wash it clean.'

God told Noah to build a very big boat. He told him exactly how it should be made. So Noah cut down trees and hammered in nails. Then he covered the boat with thick, sticky tar to keep the water out.

Everyone thought Noah was mad! 'Fancy building a boat so far from the sea,' they said.

But they would not listen when Noah told them what God was going to do.

God told Noah to take every kind of creature with him into the boat. 'Take your family with you too, ' said God. 'I will save you all from the big flood.'

15

Rain, rain and more rain

It was going to rain. Noah and his family and all the animals were safely inside the big boat, so God shut the door.

Drip! Drip! It began to rain.

Pitter-patter! The rain grew harder.

Gurgle! Splosh! The rivers burst their banks and the seas flooded the land.

Soon the boat was floating on the water. It rained and it rained for days and days till there was nothing left in the world. Everything was covered by the flood. But everyone inside the boat was safe and dry.

Many days passed. Then God sent a wind, and the waters began to go down.

Noah fetched a raven from inside the boat and set it free. But it flew round and round. There was no dry land.

Noah waited a few
days. He fetched a dove
from inside the boat and set it
free. But the big grey bird came back.
There was still no dry land.

Noah waited again. Then he sent out the dove again.
This time it came back with an olive leaf in its beak!

A few days later God told Noah it was time to leave
the boat. The animals slithered and crawled, leaped and
ran on to the dry land.

'Thank you God for keeping us safe!' said Noah.

A brightly coloured rainbow glowed in the sky.

'Look at the rainbow,' said God. 'It will remind you
that I promise never to destroy the earth with a flood
again.'

> "Dear God, thank
> you for keeping
> Noah and his family
> safe. Thank you that
> you will keep me
> safe, too."

Abraham's journey

There was once a man called Abraham who came from a city called Ur.

One day God spoke to Abraham. 'I want you to go and live in a new land,' he said. ' I will lead you on your journey and I promise that if you do as I say, I will bless you. One day, everyone will hear about you, and your family will be the start of a great nation.'

Abraham went to tell his wife, Sarah, what God had said. 'We must pack up our things and go where God leads us,' he told her. So Abraham and Sarah, and their servants and their camels and their sheep and their goats, set off on their journey.

They walked and they walked. Each night they stopped and camped in their tents.

They did not know where they

were going. But Abraham knew that God would lead them because he had promised to be with them wherever they went.

It was a long, long journey.

At last they reached the land of Canaan.

'This is the land that I will give to you and your children,' said God.

'Thank you,' said Abraham. And he put up his tent for the last time.

"Thank you, God, for being with me wherever I go."

Abraham's special son

Abraham and Sarah were
getting old. They did not have
any children. Sometimes they were sad,
but they trusted God to help them.

One day Abraham was talking to God.

'I will look after you,' God promised. 'And I will give
you more than you can imagine!'

'But what I really want is a baby boy,' Abraham told
him. 'And now we're too old to have children.'

'I promise you will have a son of your very own,' said
God. 'Look up at the sky!'

Abraham looked up. The sky was full of twinkling
stars.

20

'Can you count the stars?' asked God.

Abraham shook his head.

'Your family will be as many as the number of stars!' said God.

Abraham believed what God had said.

Some time later, Sarah had a lovely baby boy. They called him Isaac.

Abraham knew that Isaac was a very special baby. God had kept his promise.

"Thank you, God, that you never forget about the promises you make."

21

Jacob plays a trick

Abraham had two grandsons called Esau and Jacob. Even though they were twins, they were very different.

Esau was born first. When he grew up, he loved to be outdoors, running about and hunting. His father, Isaac, loved Esau best.

Jacob liked to stay at home with his mother, Rebekah. He was her favourite.

When their father was an old man, the time came for him to give his eldest son, Esau, a special blessing. This meant that Esau would be the head of the family after his father had died.

'But before I bless you, go and get some meat for a special meal,' said Isaac. So Esau went out hunting. Rebekah saw the chance for Jacob, the youngest son, to get Esau's blessing instead.

'Quick!' she said. 'I will make your father's favourite meal while you dress yourself in Esau's clothes. Wrap some animal skins around your arms, so that your skin feels hairy like Esau's. Your father will never know, and you will get his blessing!'

Jacob did what Rebekah said. He took the food, and went in to see his father.

'Is that really you, Esau?' said Isaac. He was so old, he could hardly see.

'Yes, Father,' lied Jacob. Isaac reached out and touched Jacob's arms which were covered in animal skins. They felt exactly like Esau's hairy arms.

And so Isaac gave his special blessing to Jacob, instead of to Esau.

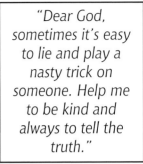

"Dear God, sometimes it's easy to lie and play a nasty trick on someone. Help me to be kind and always to tell the truth."

Joseph's jealous brothers

Jacob had a big family. He had twelve sons and one daughter. Out of all of them he loved his young son Joseph best of all.

One day, Jacob gave Joseph a very special present. It was a beautiful, brightly coloured coat.

Joseph was pleased. He wore his beautiful coat as often as he could. He liked to show it off.

Joseph's big brothers were jealous. They saw how much their father loved Joseph. They did not like Joseph's beautiful coat. They did not like Joseph, either. He was bossy and boastful.

One day, Joseph's big brothers were out working, taking care of their father's sheep.

'Go and see how your brothers are,' said his father. So Joseph set off, wearing his beautiful coat.

His brothers saw him coming.

'Here comes Joseph!' groaned one of them.

'I've had enough of him!' said another.

'Let's kill him!' said a third. 'No one will know. We could say he's been eaten by a wild animal!'

The eldest brother, Reuben, said, 'Don't kill him. Put him in this empty water-hole.'

As soon as Joseph got near, his brothers grabbed him. They tore off his beautiful coat, and threw him down into the well.

But, even at the bottom of the empty well, God was looking after him. God had plans for Joseph.

"Dear God, thank you for looking after Joseph, even though he was bossy and boastful! Thank you that you are always looking after me."

A slave in Egypt

Poor Joseph was at the bottom of an empty well. His brothers had thrown him in and left him, and they had taken his beautiful coat.

'That will teach him,' said one of them. Then the brothers sat down to eat.

'Look!' said Judah. In the distance was a long line of people and some camels. They were traders, on their way to Egypt.

'I've got a good idea!' said Judah. 'Let's sell Joseph to those traders. They will take him to Egypt to be a slave!'

The brothers were very pleased. They thought it was an excellent idea.

26

As soon as the traders came near, the brothers pulled Joseph out of the well and sold him for twenty silver coins. Then they ripped his beautiful coat, dipped it in animal blood, and went back home.

'Look what we've found!' they said to their father, showing him the coat. 'It looks like Joseph's coat!'

Jacob looked. He saw the coat. He saw the blood. 'Joseph has been killed by a wild animal,' he cried. He was very unhappy. He was sure that Joseph was dead.

But Joseph was alive. He was safe and well in Egypt. God took care of Joseph. God was with him.

"Thank you, God, that when Joseph was frightened and alone, you stayed with him. Thank you that you are with me all the time."

Let my people go!

'God's people, the Israelites, were slaves in Egypt. They had to work hard all day, making bricks in the hot sun. They wished they could leave Egypt, and go to their own land.

The baby Moses had grown up to be a man. One day, God said to him, 'My people are unhappy. I want you to be their leader. I want you to tell the king of Egypt to let them go!'

Moses did not want to be a leader. He was frightened of the king. But he did as God told him.

'God wants you to let his people go!' said Moses bravely. But the king said, 'No!'

God told Moses to hit the River Nile with his shepherd's stick. The water turned red, like blood.

'Let God's people go!' said Moses. But the king said, 'No!'

'Listen to God, or there will be trouble!' said Moses.

But the king said, 'No!'

Suddenly there were frogs in the food, frogs in the houses, frogs in the beds! Everywhere was full of frogs.

'Let God's people go, or there will be more trouble!' said Moses. But the king said, 'No!'

Soon the land of Egypt was covered in biting insects, then swarms of flies. All the cows died, and the people came out in spots. Hail fell like stones from the sky, and the crops were eaten by locusts.

Then an inky darkness covered Egypt.

'All right,' said the king. 'You can go!'

"Dear God, thank you that you see when I'm unhappy and want to help me."

The great escape

The king of Egypt changed his mind again. He would not let the Israelites go home.

God was angry. He spoke to Moses, the leader of the Israelites. 'Tell my people to get ready to leave Egypt,' he said. 'Something terrible will happen tonight, so that the king will beg you to go.'

The Israelites got ready. They packed their bags and put on their coats. They ate a special meal. God told them to paint a special sign on their houses so that they would be safe.

Then in the middle of the night, God came to Egypt. All the Israelites were safe in their houses, but in every Egyptian house something terrible happened. Some of the animals and some of the people died, including the king's son.

The king of Egypt sent for Moses. 'Take God's people, and go!' he shouted.

The Israelites left as quickly as they could. But they had not gone far, when the king of Egypt changed his mind again. 'Who will work for us now? 'he said. 'Get the chariots ready. We'll bring them back!'

The Israelites were by the Red Sea when they heard the gallop of horses and the clatter of chariots. They were trapped.

'Don't be afraid,' said Moses. 'God is with us.'

Moses stretched out his hand across the water. Suddenly a strong wind blew and made a path through the water. All the Israelites walked across on dry land until they were safe on the other side.

> "Thank you, God, that whatever happens to us, you are with us."

Samuel's sleepless night

Samuel was a very special baby. Before Samuel was born, his mother Hannah had promised that her son would serve God all his life.

So when Samuel was old enough, Hannah took him to live at Shiloh, where people came to worship God. Samuel stayed there with Eli, the priest, who looked after him and taught him all about God.

One night, Samuel was lying in bed. It was dark in the room, except for a small lamp burning dimly. Eli was asleep in another room. Everything was quiet and still.

Suddenly, Samuel heard a voice.

'Samuel!' said the voice. Samuel threw back his bed cover and got up. He went into Eli's room.

'Here I am,' he said. 'You called me.'

'No, I didn't!' said Eli. 'Go back to sleep.'

Samuel lay down. He tried to go to sleep.

'Samuel!' said the voice again. He went back to Eli.

'I didn't call you,' said Eli. 'Go back to sleep.'

'Samuel!' said the voice a third time. Samuel rushed back to Eli.

Suddenly Eli knew who was speaking to Samuel. 'God wants to speak to you,' he said. 'If you hear him again, say, "Speak to me, Lord. I'm listening."'

Samuel went back to bed.

'Samuel! Samuel!' said the voice.

Samuel took a deep breath. 'Speak to me, Lord,' he said. 'I'm listening.'

From that day, Samuel became wise and good because he listened to God.

"Dear God, thank you that you will speak to anyone who will listen. Help me to get to know your voice."

David the shepherd boy

There was once a shepherd boy called David. He lived with his father, Jesse, and his seven brothers. David's brothers were big and strong. They were tall and handsome. They were all older than David. David looked after his father's sheep.

Sometimes he frightened away lions or bears who came to steal lambs. Sometimes he killed them with a stone which he threw from his sling. David trusted God to look after him.

One day, God spoke to Samuel the prophet, his special messenger. 'Go to Bethlehem,' said God. 'I have chosen one of Jesse's sons to be the next king of Israel.'

First of all, Samuel saw Jesse's eldest son. He was big and strong. 'He would make a good king,' thought Samuel. But God said, 'He's not the one I have chosen.'

Then Samuel saw Jesse's second son. He was big and strong. 'He would make a good king,' thought Samuel. But God said, 'He's not the one I have chosen.' Samuel saw seven of Jesse's sons. They were all big and strong. They were tall and handsome. But God had not chosen any of them to be king. 'Have you any more sons?' Samuel asked Jesse.

'I'll call my youngest boy, David,' said Jesse. 'He's looking after my sheep.'

When David arrived, God said to Samuel, 'He's the one! He's not as big and strong as his brothers, but he is good, and he loves me. I have chosen David to be king.'

But Samuel and David kept it a secret for many years until the old king died.

"Thank you, God, that even though I am not big and strong, you love me, just as I am."

God looks after Elijah

God had a very special friend in the land of Israel. His name was Elijah.

In those days, the land of Israel was very, very dry. The rivers were dry and the fields were dry. There was nothing to eat and nothing to drink. It had not rained for a very long time.

'Don't worry,' said God to Elijah. 'I will look after you.'

And God told Elijah where to find a little stream. Now he had plenty to drink. He heard the flutter of wings and some birds hopped up to him. They had food in their beaks. Now he had plenty to eat.

But one day the little stream dried up.

'Don't worry,' said God to Elijah. 'I will look after you.'

And God told Elijah where to find a woman who would help him.

'Please give me something to eat,' he asked her.

'I've only got
enough for me and my
little boy,' said the woman.
    'God will look after you,' said Elijah.
'Please share your food with me.'
    So the woman took Elijah home. She made some
bread. Then she looked in the bowl. There was no more
flour. She poured out some oil. It had all gone.
    Then the woman looked again. There was plenty of
flour! The oil jar was full! She could make lots more
bread!
    'God will look after you,' said Elijah. 'You will always
have something to eat!'

"Thank you, God, for looking after Elijah. Thank you for looking after me, too."

Daniel in the lions' den

Daniel was a good man who loved God. He lived in the land of Babylon, far from his home.

Daniel was honest and worked so hard that one day the king said, 'I am going to put you in charge of my kingdom.'

But there were some bad men who lived in Babylon. The bad men grumbled. The bad men complained. The bad men did not want Daniel to be in charge. They tried to get Daniel into trouble, but Daniel would not do anything wrong. Then the bad men had an idea.

'You are such a great king!' they said to King Darius. 'Why don't you make a new law? For the next thirty days, no one is allowed to worship anyone but you. If they do, they will be thrown into a den of lions!'

So the king made the law. But Daniel worshipped God, just as he had always done, and the bad men told the king. The king was sad. The king liked Daniel, but even he could not change the law.

So Daniel was taken to the den where the lions had sharp teeth and hungry tummies. That night, the king could not sleep. In the morning, he rushed to the lions' den. 'Daniel?' he shouted.

And Daniel replied, 'I am here, my King! God sent an angel to close the lions' mouths!'

Then King Darius made a new law. 'From now on,' he said, 'everyone must worship Daniel's God!'.

"You are so powerful, Father God! Please look after me as you looked after Daniel."

The angels and the shepherds

It was the middle of the night and it was very, very dark. The stars twinkled in the sky and, huddled together in the darkness, a few poor shepherds sat on a hillside, looking after their sheep.

Suddenly a bright, bright light shone in the darkness. The shepherds were frightened.

Then a loud voice said, 'Don't be afraid!'

That made them even more frightened! They looked up into the sky and saw a bright, bright angel.

'God has sent me with some wonderful news for the whole world!' said the angel. 'A very special baby has been born in Bethlehem. He's the one God has promised who will put things right in the world. Go to Bethlehem and see him for yourselves! You will find the baby asleep in a manger.'

Suddenly the whole sky burst into light. There were angels everywhere. 'Glory to God in heaven,' they sang. 'And peace to all people on earth.'

When the angels had gone, the shepherds ran all the way to Bethlehem. They ran through the quiet streets and found the stable. Carefully they pushed open the door.

There in the stable were Mary, and Joseph, and the baby Jesus asleep in the manger.

'Thank you, God!' said the shepherds. 'We have seen your very special baby!'

"Thank you,
Father God,
that Jesus came to
help everyone
in the whole world."

The four fishermen

Jesus grew up near Lake Galilee. It was a busy place and lots of people worked there.

One day Jesus stood and watched the fishermen. Some of them were mending their nets. Others were counting their fish.

Jesus saw a little fishing boat, not far from the shore. Two of his friends were in the boat. They were throwing their nets into the water, hoping to catch some fish.

'Peter!' Jesus called. 'Andrew!'

The two brothers looked towards Jesus. They waved.

'Come with me!' called Jesus. 'Let me teach you all about God! Leave your fishing and come and be my special friends. Then you can help other people find out about God.'

Straight away Peter and Andrew dropped their nets. They jumped out of their boat, swam to the shore and went with Jesus.

"Lord Jesus, help me to follow you and learn all about God."

Jesus walked on around the lake. He saw two more brothers, James and John, sitting in their fishing boat with their father, Zebedee.

They were getting their fishing nets ready.

'Come with me!' called Jesus.

James and John jumped out of their boat, swam to the shore and went with Jesus.

The four fishermen left everything behind. They wanted to follow Jesus and learn about God.

The four kind friends

There was once a man who could not walk. He could not sit up. He could not move. He lay on a mat all day.

This man had four kind friends.

One day, the four friends heard that Jesus was visiting their town. So they took their friend to see Jesus. They were sure that Jesus could help him.

They carried the man on a mat through the town to the house where Jesus was. But everyone wanted to see Jesus! There were so many people in the house that there was no room for anyone else.

Then the four friends had an idea. Outside the house were some steps going up to the roof. Very carefully, they carried the man up the steps. Very carefully, they started to make a hole in the roof!

Everyone inside the house looked up. The four friends let the man on the mat down into the room!

Jesus looked at the four men. He knew how much they wanted to help their friend. Then he looked at the man lying on the mat. The man looked at Jesus.

'God forgives all the bad things you have done,' said Jesus. And to show this was true he did another miracle. 'Stand up! Pick up your mat and go home.'

The man sat up. The man stood up. The man bent down and picked up his mat. The man walked!

'Praise God!' he said, looking at Jesus.

Everyone was amazed. 'Praise God!' they shouted. And the man walked home.

"Dear God, thank you for friends. Help me to be a good friend to the people I know."

62

The big storm

Jesus and his friends were by Lake Galilee. It was a huge lake, almost as big as the sea.

'Let's sail across the lake,' said Jesus to his friends. They all got into the boat. It had been such a busy day!

Jesus was very tired. He lay down in the boat with his head on a pillow. Soon he fell fast asleep.

But while he was asleep the winds began to blow. The sails on the little boat flapped. The waves crashed and the boat rocked. Up and down, higher and higher. The water splashed and smashed into the little boat. It was going to sink!

Jesus' friends were very frightened. They went to Jesus and shook him awake.

'Help! We're going to drown!' they shouted.

Jesus stood up.

'Be quiet!' he shouted to the wind. The wind stopped howling.

'Be still!' he shouted to the waves. The sea grew calm.

Jesus' friends didn't know what to say. First they were excited. Then they were afraid.

'He must be very special,' they said to one another. 'Even the wind and the waves do what he says!'

> *"Thank you, Lord Jesus, that you are bigger and stronger than me. Please help me when I am afraid."*

The very big picnic

One day Jesus went into the countryside. A big crowd of people followed him. They all wanted to be with Jesus.

When evening came Jesus knew that everyone was hungry. He went to his friend Philip and asked, 'Where can we buy food for these people?'

Philip was shocked. 'For all these people?' he asked. 'It would cost far too much to buy food for everyone here!'

Just then, Jesus' friend Andrew brought a little boy to him. 'This little boy wants to give you his picnic,' he said. 'It won't do much good. He's only got five small barley rolls and two little fishes.'

Jesus smiled. 'Tell everyone to sit down,' he said.

Then Jesus took the picnic from the little boy. He picked up the barley rolls. He picked up the little fishes. 'Thank you, Father God,' he said.

Jesus gave the rolls and the fishes to his friends. His friends took some and gave the rest of rolls and the fishes to the people sitting on the grass. Everyone began to eat. There was enough for them all. There was so much food, they could not finish it!

Jesus told his friends to pick up the food that was left over. The disciples went through the crowd. They filled up twelve big baskets.

Everyone was amazed. 'Jesus must be a very special person,' they said to one another.

> "Lord Jesus, thank you that you cared for all those hungry people!"

The story of the lost sheep

One day Jesus told this story.

'Once there was a shepherd who had a hundred sheep. Every day he counted them: 1, 2, ...98, 99, 100. He knew them all. Each one of them was special.

'One day the shepherd went to count his sheep: 1, 2, ...98, 99 ...98, 99. But where was the hundredth sheep? It was missing!

'Quickly, the shepherd took his shepherd's stick and walked over the hills, looking for the sheep that was lost. He looked in the brambles and he looked on rocky ledges. He looked in the ditches and he looked under the trees. The shepherd looked everywhere. He did not give up.

'Eventually the shepherd saw the lost sheep. He ran to rescue it. He was very happy that he had found it. The shepherd picked up the little sheep, and put it on his shoulders. Carefully he carried it home.

'"Look everyone!" he said to his friends. "Let's have a party because I've found my lost sheep."

'All his friends were happy! The shepherd had found his lost sheep.'

Jesus looked at the people who were listening to him.

'This is a story about God,' he said. 'God is like that shepherd. Some of you are like the little sheep that got lost. God has come to rescue you, and when you start living to please him, God is as happy as the shepherd who found his lost sheep.'

"Dear God, thank you that you love me!"

The king on a donkey

Jesus and his friends were walking towards the big city of Jerusalem. As they got near the city, Jesus sent two of his friends to fetch a donkey from the next village.

The two friends brought the donkey to him. They put their coats on its back, and Jesus climbed on.

There were crowds of people standing by the road into Jerusalem. When they saw Jesus coming, some of them spread their coats on the road and made a path for the donkey to walk on.

80

Other people climbed up the trees.
They cut down huge palm branches and put
them on the road.

As Jesus rode by they shouted, 'King Jesus! Glory to
God who saves us!'

The crowd made so much noise and everyone was so
excited, that the people in Jerusalem heard about it long
before Jesus got there.

'What's all the fuss about?' they asked.

'Jesus is coming, the king on a donkey!' the people
replied.

And so Jesus arrived in Jerusalem.

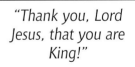

"Thank you, Lord Jesus, that you are King!"

Jesus dies

Not everyone in Jerusalem was Jesus' friend. Some people didn't like what he said about God. Some people didn't like it when he healed people. Some people wanted to stop all the crowds of people following him. 'Surely he can't be the Son of God,' they said.

These people thought of a way to get him into trouble. They told lies about him, and had him arrested. Even though Jesus had done nothing wrong, the rulers of

Jerusalem said he must die.

The Roman soldiers took Jesus and dressed him up like a king. They cut down some branches from a thorn bush, and twisted them round to make a crown. They put it on Jesus' head. Then the soldiers made fun of Jesus. 'Your majesty!' they laughed.

They made Jesus carry a huge piece of wood on his back. Then they tied it to a tree to make a cross and left him to die.

Jesus' mother, Mary, and his friends watched and waited. They were very, very sad.

After some time the earth shook and the sky turned black. Jesus cried out in a loud voice, 'Father God, I give you my life!'

And then he died.

A Roman soldier watched as Jesus died. 'This Jesus really was God's Son,' he said.

Later that day, his friends took the body of Jesus and put it in a tomb in a garden. Then they rolled a very big stone across the entrance.

"Thank you God that even though bad things happened to Jesus, it was all part of your plan."

83

Jesus is alive!

Jesus' friends were very sad because Jesus was dead.

Very early in the morning, on the third day after Jesus had died, one of Jesus' friends came to the tomb. She was called Mary Magdalene.

When Mary got there, she saw that the huge stone had been rolled away from the entrance. She looked inside. The tomb was empty! Jesus was not there.

Mary began to cry. What had happened to Jesus? She looked inside the tomb again.

Then she saw two angels. 'Why are you crying?' they asked.

'Because someone has taken Jesus away,' she sobbed.

'Why are you crying?' asked a voice.

Mary turned round. A man was standing behind her. She thought it was the gardener. 'They have taken Jesus away, and I don't know where,' she cried. 'If you have taken him, please tell me. I will go and get him.'

'Mary!' said the man.

Mary heard the voice. She knew who it was! It wasn't the gardener. It was Jesus! He was alive!

'Go and tell my friends that I am alive,' said Jesus.

Mary ran to tell Jesus' friends, 'He is alive! I have seen him with my own eyes!'

"You are alive! Thank you, Lord Jesus!"

Thomas believes

Jesus' friends had seen him, alive again. They had seen the marks on his hands and his feet where he had been hurt. Now they knew that he was alive. They were very, very happy.

Except for Thomas. He had not seen Jesus. And now he just could not believe that Jesus was alive.

'But we've seen him!' the disciples told him.

They must be dreaming, he thought.

'Unless I see and touch the nail marks for myself, I will not believe it!' said Thomas firmly.

A week after Jesus rose from the dead, all the friends met together. They locked the door. This time Thomas was with them.

Suddenly Jesus appeared. He greeted them all and then he turned to Thomas. He held out his hands.

'Come on, Thomas,' he said. 'Touch my hands. See where I was hurt. I am alive!'

Then Thomas knew that it really was Jesus. He was alive!

Thomas got down on his knees.

'My Lord and my God!' he said.

"I can't see you, Lord Jesus. Help me to know that you are real."

Jesus goes back into heaven

It was six weeks since God had brought Jesus back to life. Jesus and his friends had walked together and talked together and eaten meals together. He really was alive.

Jesus told them that he had to go away, but he promised them he would always be with them in a special way.

'I want you to tell the whole world about me, and I want you to teach people how to follow me,' he said.

'But first you must wait in Jerusalem and God will send his helper, the Holy Spirit, to be with you. Then everyone in the whole world will hear about me.'

The last time the friends saw Jesus was near the village of Bethany. They were on a hillside when a cloud came down. Suddenly Jesus had gone.

While Jesus' friends were standing there, two angels

came and stood beside them.

'Jesus has gone back to heaven,' said the angels. 'But one day he will come to earth again.'

The disciples remembered what Jesus had said. So they went to Jerusalem and waited for God to send them his helper, the Holy Spirit.

"Thank you, Lord Jesus, for sending the Holy Spirit to help me."

The good news of Jesus

On a festival day called Pentecost Jesus' friends were all together in Jerusalem. Suddenly they heard a sound like the wind. It blew through the house. Then they saw something that looked like flames, but there was no fire.

All of a sudden, the disciples didn't feel afraid any more. They knew the Holy Spirit was with them. They went out into the city to tell people all about Jesus.

There were people from all over the world staying in Jerusalem for the Feast of Pentecost and when the disciples started to speak, the visitors were amazed.

'We can understand what they are saying!' they said. 'How can they speak so many different languages?'

So Peter stood up and said, 'God has done something wonderful today. He has given us his Holy Spirit, a sign that God is with us. 'And he told them all about Jesus.

'If you say sorry to God for the wrong things you have done,' said Peter, 'and believe in Jesus, then you can be God's friend.'

On that day 3,000 people became friends of Jesus. They shared the things they had with each other, and they met together to pray and to praise God. Many people were healed.

Soon the good news of Jesus spread out from Jerusalem to other countries. And 2,000 years later, there are friends of Jesus all over the world.

"Thank you, Jesus, for being my friend."